Ireland

Books by W.A. Poucher
available from Constable

Scotland
Wales
The Lake District
The Highlands of Scotland
The Alps
The Yorkshire Dales
  and the Peak District
Lakeland fells
The West Country
Skye
The magic of Skye
The Scottish Peaks
The Peak and Pennines
The Lakeland Peaks
The Welsh Peaks

Other books now out of print

The backbone of England
Climbing with a camera
Escape to the hills
A camera in the Cairngorms
Scotland through the lens
Highland holiday
The North Western Highlands
Lakeland scrapbook
Lakeland through the lens
Lakeland holiday
Lakeland journey
Over lakeland fells
Wanderings in Wales
Snowdonia through the lens
Snowdon holiday
Peak panorama
The Surrey hills
The magic of the Dolomites
West country journey
Journey into Ireland

25th Dec 1995

I hope you enjoy this beautiful book Liam.
Love,
Máire

Constable London

IRELAND

W.A. Poucher

First published in Great Britain 1986
by Constable and Company Limited
10 Orange Street London WC2H 7EG
Copyright © 1986 by W.A. Poucher
ISBN 0 09 466850 7
Text filmset by Servis Filmsetting Ltd, Manchester
Printed and bound in Japan by
Dai Nippon Company, Tokyo

The photographs

Preface

Every traveller in search of beauty is confronted by the problem of selection because there are so many lovely places in this world and life is not long enough to see them all. My own preference has always been for the wild places such as mountains, lonely valleys and splendid sea-cliffs. After seeing and photographing most of those in Britain, as well as many in Europe and America, I turned a longing eye towards Ireland, to see how its landscapes and seascapes compared with theirs; and spent four months exploring the remotest and most picturesque regions, and climbing the most interesting mountains. After driving over the greater part of the Emerald Isle, I was full of praise for its charms, particularly those of its fine western seaboard which is always beautiful and in places attains to the spectacular.

The colourful glories of the great mountains of Kerry, Connemara and Donegal have to be seen to be believed; and in the latter two areas innumerable sedgy blue lochans, dappling the boggy moorland, add a mystic charm to the mountain approaches. As for the world-famous beauty of Killarney, only those who have not seen its lakes at their best, with smooth surfaces reflecting sun-drenched woods and white woolly clouds, can think it over-rated.

However, to see all this scenery displayed to perfection requires good weather, which is the one great gamble when taking a holiday – and nowhere more so than in Erin! Owing to its situation in the path of the Gulf Stream warm air sweeps over this land of mountains with such persistence and force that condensation of the clouds, and consequent rain, are inevitable. I spent May and June of two consecutive years waiting for my chance to capture these pictures, and was frequently delayed by rain – alternatively, by impenetrable heat-haze.

This is my first book of Irish pictures in colour, and I hope that after reading it tourists of every nationality will be tempted to follow in my footsteps and explore Ireland for themselves. The pictures are arranged as a circular tour, starting just outside Dublin, and the captions mention some of the best centres from which to visit the different regions, as well as the most rewarding viewpoints for the loveliest vistas in this delightful island.

W.A. Poucher
1986

Bray Head and the Sugarloaf from the hill of Howth

The Sugarloaf is an outlier of the Wicklow
Mountains, whose granite domes cover the
largest area of high ground in Ireland, and
whose highest summit, Lugnaquillia, is
surpassed only by the giants of Kerry.

The Round Tower, Glendalough

Glendalough is perhaps the most frequented valley in the Wicklow Mountains, and the first thing to catch the visitor's eye on entering the glen is the ancient Round Tower, 103 ft high. It stands in the corner of an immense graveyard, along with other ruins of the ancient monastic settlement of St Kevin.

Glenmalure

(overleaf)

This exceptionally straight valley occupies the line of a geological fault: on a fine summer's day its floor is aglow with gorse, and the River Avonbeg gleams like a polished aquamarine.

Coumshingaun

The showpiece of the grand, broken front of the
Comeragh Mountains is the great corrie of
Coumshingaun (which means 'corrie of the
ants'). Its huge cliffs encircle a stygian tarn,
whose shores are littered with rocks and
boulders.

The Knockmealdown Mountains from Kilcoran Lodge

(overleaf)

The whole of this range, which extends for some 14 miles, is good walking country. The rounded heathery domes of these mountains are dominated by Knockmealdown (2,609 ft), and are crossed by an excellent road at the Vee (right of centre).

Galtymore from Knockeenatoung

At 3,018 ft, Galtymore is Ireland's highest
inland mountain, and rewards the energetic
walker with a superb panorama in all directions.

The *summit of* Galtymore
(overleaf)

In 1932 a large stone cross was erected on this dominating peak of the Galtees range, to commemorate the 1,500th anniversary of the landing of St Patrick in Ireland. It, and the subsequent iron and stone crosses (such as the one in the picture), fell victim to the weather: at present it is crowned by an iron Celtic cross put up in 1975.

Gouganebarra

I took this picture many years ago, looking west
from near the head of Gouganebarra Lake in
remote County Cork. Owing to extensive
afforestation schemes, this view now looks very
different.

The Sugarloaf from Bantry Bay

(overleaf)

The tortuous road that runs along the shore of Bantry Bay and through Glengarriff (reputed to be the most beautiful village in County Cork) unfolds an enchanting view of the Sugarloaf (1,887 ft) – one of several mountains in Ireland to bear this name.

Calvary on Healy Pass

The road from Adrigole to Lauragh in the rugged Beara Peninsula twists and turns across the Caha Mountains, with numerous hairpin bends that reminded me of roads in the Alps or Dolomites. This beautiful white Calvary group is on the Cork side of the pass, just before you reach the ridge crest and cross into the kingdom of Kerry.

The Iveragh Mountains from the crest of Healy Pass

(overleaf)

The sudden revelation of the Iveragh Mountains stretching across the skyline, with the Kenmare River far below, is the highlight of the journey through the savage country round Healy Pass, and should not be missed by visitors to this lovely region.

Composing a colour picture

The brilliant gold of the gorse in the foreground
contrasts perfectly with the purple of the distant
Iveragh Mountains and the white of the cloud-
masses above them.

The Reeks from Windy Gap

(overleaf)

Beyond the village of Kenmare the road rises gradually to Windy Gap, which discloses a grand panorama of Macgillicuddy's Reeks. From here a turn to the right takes one downhill all the way to Killarney.

Evening clouds on Mangerton

On the way to Killarney there is a superb view of the great curving whaleback of Mangerton (2,756 ft). This mountain is a magnet for walkers and climbers. It is easily reached from Killarney up a path starting near the Muckross House car-park.

The Reeks from the east

(overleaf)

One of the best views of the magnificent jagged ridge of Macgillicuddy's Reeks is from the road that runs along the south-east side of Upper Lake on its way to Killarney.

The Killarney lakes

There are several excellent vantage points for
the appraisal of this luxuriant valley, but I think
this is the best of them – just beyond
Looscaunagh Lough, where the ground drops
away suddenly and the string of lakes is revealed
far below. It is a fitting conclusion to one of the
most dramatic journeys in the Emerald Isle.

Eagles' Nest

(overleaf)

The blue waters of Lough Leane make an
excellent foreground for the bulk of Eagles'
Nest, which looms over them: this picture was
taken from the Long Range to the south-east.

Torc Mountain

This little pyramid of Torc stands out against
the sky with dramatic clarity when seen from
the boat-landing on Lough Leane.

Ross Castle

(overleaf)

A perfect still day gave me the clear atmosphere and good lighting needed for this superb picture of the fifteenth-century ruins of Ross Castle, reflected in the mirror of Lough Leane.

Shehy Mountain

Mountains rise all around the huge sheet of
water that is Lough Leane; looking west-south-
west across it, there is a splendid view of Shehy
Mountain (right) and craggy Eagles' Nest (left).

Shehy Mountain from the north-east

(overleaf)

Seen from one of the landing-places near the
Killarney Golf Course, whose smooth fairways
border the northern shore of Lough Leane,
Shehy Mountain is backed by the fine, bold
profiles of Purple and Tomies Mountains.

Killarney at sundown

The beauty of Killarney is world-famous: my
favourite picture is this which I took between
six and seven o'clock one evening, when mellow
sunlight and drifting clouds transformed the still
lake into one of the most perfect scenes it has
been my good fortune to witness.

The gardens at Muckross House

One of the most popular attractions within easy reach of Killarney is Muckross House, with extensive gardens, a lovely rockery of soapstone, and masses of colourful azaleas and rhododendrons clustered beneath the stately pines. The Demesne forms the kernel of Killarney National Park, which stretches from Killarney to the Upper Lake, and from Purple Mountain to Mangerton.

Beenkeragh and Skregmore

(overleaf)

The magnificent, undulating ridge of the Reeks is the chief glory of the Kerry hills, and the traverse of its whole crest is perhaps the grandest ridge walk in Ireland. This picture shows the western end of the ridge, with Skregmore (right) and Beenkeragh (centre).

The eastern Reeks from Hag's Glen

The Reeks are formed mainly of Old Red
Sandstone, and this photograph shows their
serrated eastern ridge to advantage. On the left
is Cruach Mhor, while to the extreme right can
be seen the saddle to which rises the
conspicuous rock gully known as the Devil's
Ladder.

Carrauntoohil

Carrauntoohil is the monarch of Ireland's mountains, rearing 3,414 ft above sea-level and affording a stupendous panorama which reaches to the distant Atlantic if the atmosphere is clear. This picture was taken from the Hag's Glen, which is the easiest approach to it.

The summit of Carrauntoohil

(overleaf)

By the cairn on the lonely, snow-swept summit
of Carrauntoohil stands a large cross: today it is
a steel one, but this picture shows the wooden
one which preceded it.

Caher

(overleaf, pp 66/67)

From the lofty summit of Carrauntoohil, you
descend to a saddle, and then climb the
sensational knife-edge to the summit of Caher
(3,200 ft), with steep cliffs plummeting down
to Coumloughra on the right, 1,700 ft below.

Kerry sunshine

Part of the charm of walking in the Emerald Isle
is the fickleness of the weather – on a sunny
day, with blue skies and sailing white clouds,
the visitor feels fortunate indeed. But beware –
clouds or mist can roll in within moments, and
completely change the picture!

Brandon

This mountain occupies a superb situation overhanging the Atlantic on the north side of the end of Dingle Peninsula. It has two well defined tops – Brandon Mountain (right) and Brandon Peak (left), between which two rock-bound corries (clearly visible in the picture) cradle a chain of small lakes.

The falls of Ennistimmon

(overleaf)

These famous falls cascade down over broad ledges of rock and make a charming picture in the evening, with sunlight glinting on the water and the village houses behind them.

The cliffs of Moher

These breathtaking cliffs form a sheer
precipitous wall rising 668 ft above the waves
and fronting the Atlantic for 5 miles. Every
visitor to Erin should make a point of viewing
this wonderful seascape. O'Brien's Tower,
which crowns the northernmost promontory, is
the principal viewpoint (*see overleaf*).

View from O'Brien's Tower

(overleaf)

In the late afternoon the line of cliffs is well illuminated and the view from the Tower shows them at their best, the limitless sea glittering like diamonds in the lowering sunlight.

O'Brien's Tower and Goat Island

The slender stack of rock rising from the sea is
known as Goat Island. The Tower is named
after Cornelius O'Brien who owned this land
some 150 years ago, and who built both the
road that runs parallel with the cliffs, and the
Tower which is now in ruins.

Approach to the hills of Connemara

(overleaf)

The landscape round the road from Galway changes like magic around the village of Oughterard as the outlines of the Twelve Bens and the Maumturks are first seen on the horizon. Their graceful contours and the vivid colouring of the landscape are part of the charm of the 'Golden West'.

The Maumturk Mountains

My first drive in Connemara was along a wild
hill road above Lough Inagh (seen in this
picture) which opened up a magnificent view of
the hazy and mysterious Maumturk range.
Today, much of the foreground of the picture is
forested.

Ballynahinch Castle

(overleaf)

This lovely castle, formerly the home of 'Ranji', HH the Jam Sahib of Nawanaga, is now transformed into an hotel. It is dominated by Benlettery, an imposing conical peak which is the southern outpost of the Twelve Bens.

Salmon river at Ballynahinch

Ballynahinch is a favourite with fishermen, and
an excellent centre from which to explore the
rivers, loughs and tidal inlets of remote and
beautiful Connemara.

Benbreen and Bengower

(overleaf)

The Twelve Bens are a rocky mass of mountains whose hard, smooth quartzite summits have little or no vegetation. This view of two of the peaks – Benbreen (centre) and Bengower (left) – is taken from the Recess–Clifden road at the west end of Derryclare Lough.

The ridge walk

The finest ridge walk over the Twelve Bens
includes this stretch from Derryclare to Ben
Corr (which is the massive two-headed peak in
the middle ground). In the background is the
long crest of the Mweelrea Mountains.

The view from Derryclare

On attaining the lofty cairn of Derryclare, I
found it to be a much better viewpoint than the
tops to the west. It disclosed a silent, stony
wilderness in which the peaks of Muckanaght,
Benbaun and Bencollaghduff were splendidly
etched against the sky.

Benbreen

(overleaf)

The summit of Benbreen (2,276 ft) is separated from Derryclare (whence I took this picture) by the deep Glencoaghan valley. Care needs to be taken when walking along these ridges, as the rocks, especially when wet, are very slippery, and cliffs fall precipitously into the valley.

The view from Benlettery

My first attempt on the Twelve Bens was made from Benlettery, and I found the ridge from there to Bengower (right, middle ground) easy going: but on attaining the summit of Bengower and seeing the immense drop to the col between it and Benbreen (left, background) I decided to spend a pleasant hour resting and enjoying the view. Then I returned to my car via the spacious, deserted, River Owenglin valley, which since then has been extensively planted with State forests.

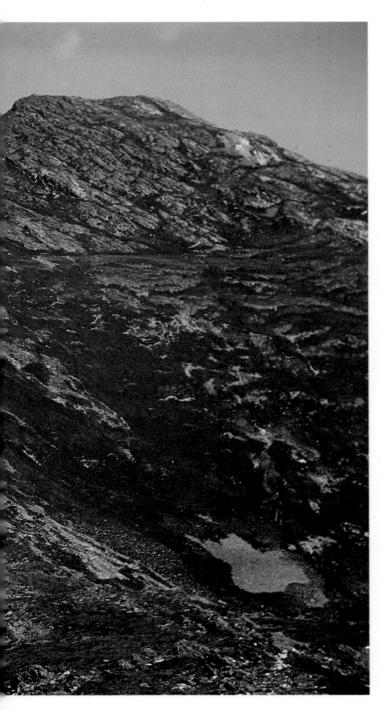

Three of the Twelve

(overleaf)

The road that runs near the western end of Ballynahinch Lake yields a superb view of three tops in the imposing Twelve Bens group – Benlettery (right), Ben Glenisky (centre), and Ben Cullagh (left, background).

Connemara landscape

(overleaf, pp 100/101)

This wild region, with its secluded valleys, its innumerable lochans and occasional white-painted cottages set against the backdrop of frowning mountains and changing cloudscapes, is the photographer's delight.

The Twelve Bens from Clifden

The two conspicuous spires of Clifden signal the
visitor's arrival in the capital of Connemara,
with its superb backdrop of the Twelve Bens
group.

Cashel Bay

(overleaf)

The enchanting, fretted south-western coastline of Connemara, with its aquamarine waters and boulders draped with orange wrack, gives distant glimpses of the Twelve Bens to the north.

Connemara cottage

This cottage was the dwelling house of a
Connemara small farmer when I photographed it
thirty years ago. Now almost all these thatched
stone cottages are roofless ruins, or else used to
shelter cattle.

View from the road to Roundstone

(overleaf)

Driving on from Cashel Bay, skirting the many rocky sea inlets, I took this picture of the purple-shadowed mass of the Twelve Bens to the north – the little fishing-boat makes a perfect foreground.

Roundstone harbour

This little fishing village, whose cottages
overlook the tiny harbour, was one of the
prettiest spots I visited – I lingered there for an
hour, chatting with the fishermen and admiring
the splendid skyline of the Bens.

Kylemore Abbey
(overleaf)

This huge, imposing mock-Elizabethan building of limestone-faced granite stands on the northern shore of Lough Poolacappul, immediately below the stony slopes of Doughruagh: though formerly a residence, it is now a school supervised by Benedictine sisters.

The rocky eastern front of the Maumturks

The road to Cong from Maum Bridge threads a
delightful landscape, with the rounded bulk of
the Maumturks on the skyline and stretches of
Lough Corrib in the foreground.

Aasleagh falls

(overleaf)

On the side road to Delphi I paused to admire the waterfall on the River Erriff at Aasleagh. It makes a charming picture with the steeply falling ridges of the Partry Mountains behind it.

Fin Lough in the Delphi Valley

In the narrow gash between Mweelrea and
Bengorm, backed by the Sheeffrey Mountains,
this lovely spot reminded an eighteenth-century
Lord Sligo, just back from the Grand Tour, of
Delphi in Greece. Further upstream, tiny Fin
Lough is guarded by hills and trees.

Croagh Patrick

(overleaf)

This shapely mountain, known more familiarly as 'the Reek', is the most beautiful in Ireland. This photograph, which perfectly reveals its noble form, is taken from above Westport.

St Patrick's Monument on Croagh Patrick

Croagh Patrick rises immediately to the south of
Clew Bay, and reaches a height of 2,510 ft. Its
ascent is made by the broad and stony Pilgrim's
Track which starts beside the hotel in Murrisk,
and as you climb an increasingly beautiful view
unfolds behind you.

The oratory on the summit

On the last Sunday in July each year, Croagh Patrick is ascended by a host of pilgrims, many barefoot, whose journey ends at this little oratory. Here they honour St Patrick, who supposedly banished all the snakes in Ireland from this spot. The picture also yields a distant glimpse of Clare Island.

View from the summit
(overleaf)

On a clear day, the panorama unfolded from the summit of Croagh Patrick is undoubtedly the finest in all Ireland. It reveals the gleaming blue of Clew Bay, studded with innumerable islets, and backed by the Mayo ranges from Glennamong to Nephin.

Distant prospect
(overleaf, pp. 128/129)

Across the azure waters of Clew Bay is the little village of Mallaranny, backed by low hills.

The Curraun Peninsula

A clear atmosphere and a combination of sun
and cloud transforms both landscape and
seascape into pictures of serene beauty that are
any photographer's dream. This peninsula is the
gateway to Achill Island.

Slievemore from Dugort

(overleaf)

Achill Island is the largest off the coast of
Ireland, and is famed for its fine cliff scenery
and lovely sandy bays. From Dugort,
Slievemore is seen in splendid elevation, its
contours tapering gracefully to a conical top,
and overlooking the little yellow strand.

County Mayo cottage

(overleaf, pp 134/135)

Notice the stones to hold down the thatch —
they are necessary because of the Atlantic gales
which sweep this lonely island.

Croaghaun from Dooagh

Croaghaun rises 2,192 ft on the extreme west of
Achill Island, and its seaward side is cliff-bound
almost up to its lofty summit. However, I had a
disappointing search for a viewpoint of these
cliffs, and concluded that they would be best
seen from a boat about a mile out to sea!

The Menawn cliffs
(overleaf)

Menawn is the third peak on Achill Island, though at 1,530 ft it is considerably lower than Slievemore (2,204 ft) and Croaghaun. It overlooks Keel, and its long line of sheer-falling cliffs makes a sensational picture when seen across the bay.

Benbulbin from the west
(overleaf, pp 140/141)

On driving north from Sligo, Benbulbin is among the first tops of the Dartry Mountains to catch the eye, jutting out like the prow of a titanic ship, and rimmed on three sides by perpendicular cliffs.

Cottage below Benbulbin

I was particularly attracted by the Dartry
Mountains and spent a couple of sunny days
exploring the adjacent moorland and looking for
the best viewpoints for their photography. This
immaculate cottage made a perfect foreground
for the majestic profile of Benbulbin.

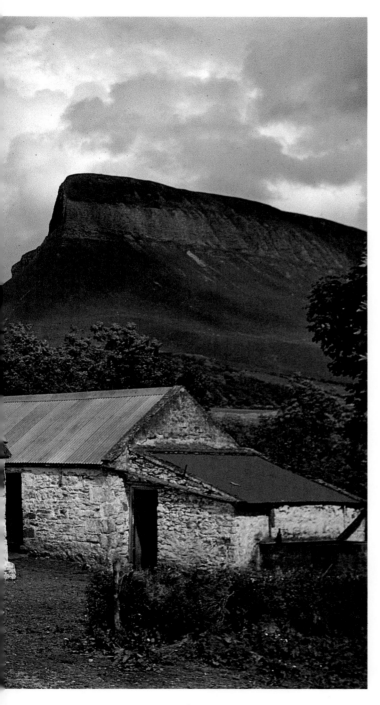

Benwhiskin

(overleaf)

Some three miles to the north of Benbulbin, the twisting Dartry ridge terminates in the magnificent curving peak of Benwhiskin, the narrowest spur of the range, whose end falls almost to the doors of the quaint cottages in the remote hamlet of Ballaghnakillick.

The main cliffs of Slieve League

The brown mountains on the northern side of
Donegal Bay culminate in the mighty form of
Slieve League, whose two miles of steep cliffs
fall in one swoop into the Atlantic Ocean.
Remarkable as their immensity is, it is their
subtle variation of colour that adds so much to
their scenic grandeur.

The Derryveagh Mountains from the south-west

(overleaf)

Driving north through Donegal, from Ardara to Dunglow, I found the countryside enlivened by sedgy lochans to the right and by lovely stretches of Trawenagh Bay to the left, until on the skyline I caught my first glimpse of the distant Derryveagh Mountains.

Errigal and Aghla More

(overleaf, pp 150/151)

Errigal (right), rising 2,466 ft into the sky as a gleaming white pyramid, is the most majestic of Donegal's mountains: since it consists mostly of white quartzite it presents an alluring picture on a sunny afternoon. The peak on the left is Aghla More.

The Poisoned Glen

This celebrated valley is the Derryveagh Mountains' most remarkable feature and the strangest place I visited in Ireland. It is flanked by boiler-plated, greyish-white, granite cliffs like the sides of a gigantic fortress. The valley, which probably derives its name from the Irish Spurge, a highly toxic plant that used to grow there, has at its entrance the ruins of a lonely church.

Lough Veagh

(overleaf)

Lough Veagh is the most beautiful lake in
Ireland – a narrow sheet of water 4 miles long,
enclosed by rugged hills, with tall pines standing
sentinel near the road running past its outlet.
This valley is now a National Park.

Muckish

(overleaf, pp 156/157)

This lovely view of Muckish is taken from the
north-east across Sheep Haven when the tide
was low.

The great cliffs of Horn Head

Horn Head is a grand promontory immediately
to the north of Dufanaghy: its cliffs are more
than 600 ft high in places, and plunge dizzyingly
into the sea. I enjoyed the windy walk around
their northern arc, with the surging tide far
below.

Horn Head from the Rosguil Peninsula

(overleaf)

The famed Atlantic Drive encircles Rosguil Peninsula and reveals some of the loveliest seascapes in Donegal. The most striking prospect, seen in the morning light, is of the cliffs at Horn Head, with Tory Island on the far horizon.

Cottages at Dundooan

The Atlantic Drive is about 9 miles long: it is a moot point as to which is the best way to do it, east to west, or west to east. But as it is of no great length, perhaps the solution is to make the circuit twice, travelling from the east in the morning and from the west in the evening, so as to see the views with every advantage of light and colour.

White Arch
near Portrush

The Antrim Coast Road which runs for 85 miles from Portrush to Belfast is one of the finest marine drives in Europe. The grand cliff scenery owes much of its beauty to an extraordinary combination of dazzling white limestone, black basalt, and red sandstone. Not far from Portrush the road passes the White Rocks, of which this Arch is a principal feature.

The ruins of
Dunluce Castle

(overleaf)

The picturesque towers and gables of ruined Dunluce Castle lie a few miles further along the road from Portrush, perched unassailably on a projecting rock of black basalt. Originally built about 1300 by the Norman-Irish Richard de Burgo, it defied all besiegers until 1584. Even after that it was a refuge for some Spaniards from the Armada, who were sent on to Scotland by the castle's owner, 'Sorley Boy' MacDonnell.

The Giant's
Causeway (centre)
and Plaiskin
Head from above

(overleaf, pp 168/169)

A splendid circular walk from the cliff-top car-park takes you down to the Grand Causeway, on past the Wishing Chair and other formations, near to the site of the Armada ship *Girona*, and finally up a wooden staircase at Benbane Head, whence a path leads back to the car-park.

Plaiskin Head from the Causeway

The Giant's Causeway ranks with Fingal's Cave
on Staffa as one of the wonders of the natural
world, and the remarkable basaltic formations
are easier of access and can be more closely
examined here than those of the Hebridean
island.

Portnaboe from the Causeway

The vertical basaltic formations may be of
surpassing interest to geologists, but to the
ordinary visitor they depend more for their
appeal upon the fancy names given to the
groups of pentagonal and hexagonal columns
(*see overleaf*).

The Wishing Chair

(overleaf)

This mound of basaltic pillars only resembles a 'wishing chair' with much imaginative thinking on the part of the viewer!

Bengore Head

(overleaf, pp 176/177)

On approaching Balintoy there is this noble retrospect of the coastline, dominated by Bengore Head, with the Atlantic rollers breaking on the gleaming sands of White Park Bay – a seascape of real splendour.

The swinging bridge

Carrick-a-Rede is a basalt stack beyond Balintoy, connected with the mainland only by this flimsy-looking bridge of rope and boards, which crosses a channel through which heavy seas surge 80 ft below.

Fairhead

(overleaf)

This mighty headland comes into view again and again on the road to Ballycastle: this is the first view of it from the west. It completely dominates the coast hereabouts, with its crest 636 ft above the waves and its upper half consisting of a spectacular sheer cliff of columnar basalt.

Cushendun

(overleaf, pp 182/183)

This quaint village nestles at the mouth of Glendun, and has such charm and atmosphere that it is a great favourite with artists as well as cameramen.

Garron Point

The fine marine drive runs along the rim of Red
Bay, which is hemmed in by sandstone cliffs and
is a jewel of the Antrim coast. From here there
is a superb view of the broken white chalk cliffs
of Garron Point.

Carrickfergus Castle

The last interesting feature of the drive before
Belfast is the grand Norman castle of
Carrickfergus, which dominates the town of that
name. Standing on a sea-girt, rocky peninsula, it
was probably built late in the twelfth century,
and was garrisoned as recently as 1928.

The Mountains of Mourne

(overleaf)

The Mournes, famous in song and story, stretch from Newcastle to Newry. Their three chief peaks – from left to right Slieve Bearnagh, Slieve Binnian and Slieve Donard – are seen here from Kilkeel.

Slieve Donard

'Sweeping down to the sea', Slieve Donard at
2,796 ft, is the highest peak of the Mournes –
indeed, the highest peak in Ulster. It is seen here
from the Royal County Down Golf Links.

Slieve Bearnagh and Slieve Meelmore

(overleaf)

Though Slieve Donard is the highest of the Mournes, it is Slieve Bearnagh (left) with its castellated summit and two rocky tors, which holds the eye.

Cottages in the Mournes

(overleaf, pp 194/195)

These cottages and drystone walls are typical features of the countryside near Annalong.

The Mourne Wall

This great boundary wall, 5 ft high in most places, which climbs to the summit of Slieve Donard, was erected by the Belfast Water Commissioners to define their catchment area.

Slieve Binnian

(overleaf)

The rocky cone of Slieve Binnian is seen to advantage from Annalong to the south-east, whose charming little harbour nestles among the picturesque cottages of the village.

Kilkeel harbour

The masts and rigging of the bright little boats
in Kilkeel harbour make a fine geometric
foreground for the superb skyline of Slieve
Binnian, with Slieve Donard to the right.

Boats at anchor

Bright paintwork and coiled ropes make a
pleasing study when the eye is surfeited with the
grandeur of far horizons.

Sunset over the Irish sea

(overleaf)

Chance can often play a big part in capturing a
good picture: in this case, I was lucky to have
my camera close at hand, so I could take the
shot before the brilliant colours faded.